WELCOME TO LINLITHGOW PALACE

Linlithgow Palace is one of the most important buildings to survive from late-medieval Scotland. Following a devastating fire in 1424, James I ordered the building of a new palace on an ambitious scale.

Subsequent kings left their own marks on the palace, and it took almost 200 years to achieve its final form. As a comfortable residence and an impressive setting for courtly display, it played a key role in the functions and presentation of royalty.

By 1600, the palace was in decline, and the north range collapsed in 1607, prompting its reconstruction as a fine domestic suite on the orders of James VI. Another fire struck in 1746, during the last Jacobite Rising, but this majestic royal palace still bears witness to the grand ambitions of the Stewart monarchs.

Above: The vaulted ceiling of the 'queen's turnpike', one of four spiral stairs added by James IV around 1500.

Opposite: Inside James IV's spacious wine cellar in the west range.

CONTENTS

HIGHLIGHTS

INSIDE THE PALACE

◀ THE FOUNTAIN
A flamboyant celebration of Renaissance kingship, James V's fountain dominates the courtyard, visible from all parts of the palace (p.11).

◀ QUEEN MARGARET'S BOWER
At the top of the queen's turnpike at the palace's north-west corner is a small room with superb views, traditionally associated with Margaret Tudor, wife of James IV (p.20).

◀ THE KING'S ORATORY
Installed by the devout James IV, this little private chapel with its oriel window provided a quiet refuge for prayer with a view over the loch (p.19).

◀ THE MUSEUM
A small but intriguing display of some of the artefacts discovered at the palace, as well as portraits of some of the monarchs who lived here (p.15).

OUTSIDE THE PALACE

◀ THE LOCH AND PEEL
Linlithgow Loch is well known for its wildlife, and for the leisure activities taking place around its shores. But the peel also has a history stretching back further than the palace itself (pp.28–31).

◀ THE EAST ENTRANCE
The original main entrance to the palace was in use from the 1420s until the 1530s. Its splendid decoration was designed to announce the sophistication and importance of the palace's royal occupants (p.26).

▲ SCULPTURE AND CARVINGS
The palace's masonry is embellished in many places – look out for a statue of the Virgin, unicorn ceiling bosses, musical angels and a boozy butler (pp.9, 14, 19 and 23).

▲ FIREPLACES
Besides two giant kitchen fireplaces, three decorated fireplaces have survived in good condition (pp.13, 18 and 21).

▲ PEDIMENTS
The courtyard windows of the north façade are surmounted by pediments decorated in honour of James VI, though he had long since abandoned Scotland to reign in England (p.10).

◄ THE OUTER GATEWAY
When James V moved the entrance to the south range in 1535, he added an archway 30m to the south, embellishing it with heraldic motifs to declare his importance and his international allegiances (p.27).

LINLITHGOW PALACE AT A GLANCE

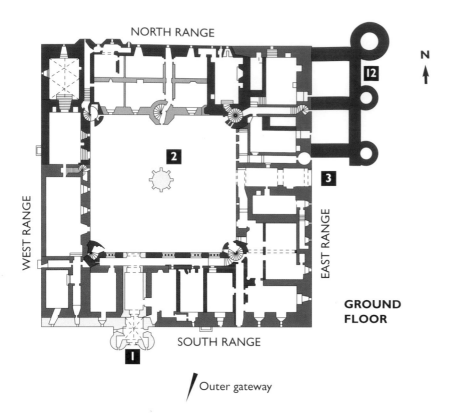

NORTH RANGE

WEST RANGE

EAST RANGE

SOUTH RANGE

N

GROUND FLOOR

Outer gateway

Linlithgow Palace's elevated, lochside location was the site of a royal residence as early as the 1100s. David I (1124–53) was the first monarch to build a residence here; he also founded the town that developed alongside it. In 1424 a great fire swept through Linlithgow, and James I (1406–37) began the task of rebuilding a great palace.

James I's great hall, although later remodelled, still dominates the east quarter of the palace. Over the course of the next century and more, James's heirs completed the building, creating an impressive quadrangular palace, with four ranges grouped around a central courtyard, and James V's magnificent fountain forming its centrepiece. Royal apartments and a royal chapel added by James IV overlook the courtyard on the south and west sides, and on the north side stands James VI's fine Renaissance range.

The loch and peel provide an attractive setting for what is arguably the most impressive of Scotland's medieval palaces.

1 SOUTH ENTRANCE

The present entrance to the courtyard was a late addition, installed around 1535 by James V. The outer gateway was also built at this time.

2 FOUNTAIN

Added by James V around 1538, the fountain is designed to signify the power, sophistication and benevolence of the king. The fountain was conserved in 2000–05 and is fully functional. Ask site staff about seasonal demonstrations.

3 EAST ENTRANCE

The original entrance, built in the 1420s. This was a key feature of James I's palace: both inside and outside were lavishly decorated with stone carvings, some of which survive.

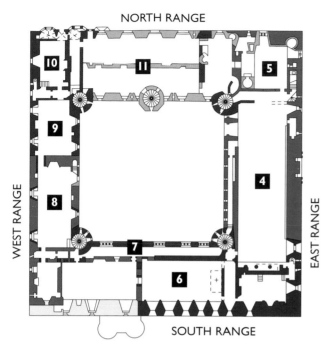

NORTH RANGE

WEST RANGE

EAST RANGE

SOUTH RANGE

**FIRST
FLOOR**

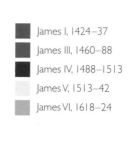

James I, 1424–37

James III, 1460–88

James IV, 1488–1513

James V, 1513–42

James VI, 1618–24

4 GREAT HALL

The main reception room, built as part of James I's original palace, with a magnificent fireplace and dais window added by James IV around 1500.

5 COURT KITCHEN

A well-appointed kitchen adjoining the great hall, where feasts were prepared.

6 CHAPEL

Added in the 1490s, the chapel probably replaced the original royal apartments. Stone carvings survive around its fine, tall windows.

7 MUSEUM

A display of artefacts found at the palace, together with portraits of some of the royal inhabitants.

8 KING'S HALL

The first and most public chamber of the king's lodgings, a sequence of three first-floor rooms in the west range, added by James IV around 1500.

9 PRESENCE CHAMBER

The second, more intimate chamber of the king's lodgings, where James might receive more privileged visitors.

10 BEDCHAMBER

The most private room of the king's lodgings would have been dominated by a large bed but may not have been used for sleeping.

11 NORTH RANGE

The most recent addition to the palace, completed around 1620. The present north range was commissioned by James VI after a previous north range built by James IV collapsed in 1607. It was badly damaged in the fire of 1746.

12 BARBICAN

Added by James IV around 1495, the barbican or forework provided additional defences around what was still the palace's main entrance. It may also have enhanced the grandeur of the entrance.

THE DEVELOPMENT OF THE PALACE

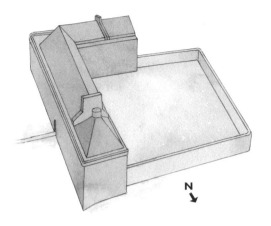

I JAMES I (1424–37)

When a great fire destroyed much of Linlithgow in 1424, James I took the opportunity to build in its place a state-of-the-art palace for the royal Stewarts. He built the east range, with a glorious entrance at its centre. Behind, on the upper floor, was the great hall, one of the finest medieval interiors in Scotland. This was flanked by kitchens (to the north) and royal lodgings (to the south and west).

We do not know whether the palace courtyard was enclosed at this date, though it would be very surprising if it was not, on both security and etiquette grounds. It is possible that not all of the old castle was destroyed in the 1424 fire, and that part of it remained in use, to the west of James's new east range. James spent some days at Linlithgow in 1428, perhaps in this 'old' part, whilst observing progress on his new pleasure palace.

2 JAMES III (1460–88)

James II (1437–60) appears to have contributed little to his father's grand project. It was James I's grandson, James III, who probably demolished what was left of the old castle and extended the royal lodgings in the south range further west and north. The palace now started to take on its enclosed quadrangular form. Tall towers also began to appear at this point (James I's palace seems not to have had any), including the lofty south-west tower.

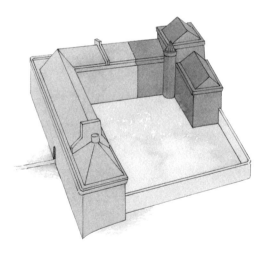

3 JAMES IV (1488–1513)

James IV effectively completed his father's
courtyard, by extending the west range
northwards and linking it to a new north range.
These two ranges together served as upgraded
royal lodgings. The former royal lodgings in the
south range were converted into a royal chapel.
A three-tiered gallery built along the south side
of the courtyard provided sheltered corridors
between the great hall and the royal lodgings.
Four turnpike stairs, one in each corner of the
courtyard, provided vertical access to all areas.
On the outside, a barbican, or gun-defence,
was built at the north end of the east range.
Intended perhaps more for show than for
military intent, it also acted as buttressing
at this weak point of the palace.

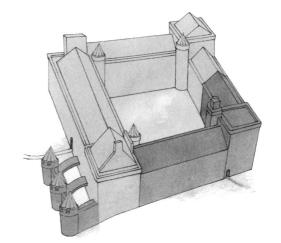

4 JAMES V (1513–42)

James V's contribution was more cosmetic, but no
less significant. He created a new entrance from
the south, including the new outer gateway at
the top of the Kirkgate, to complement the east
entrance, which retained its role as ceremonial
entry. This heightened focus on the south front
made James recast it to make it appear symmetrical,
by straightening the wall line and building
matching corner towers. He also enhanced
the courtyard with an exquisite fountain.

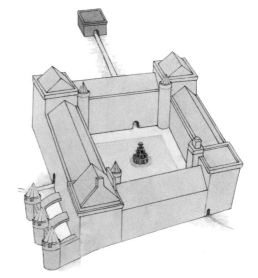

5 JAMES VI (1567–1625)

James VI's contribution was forced upon him,
following the collapse of the north range in 1607.
He rebuilt it on a pattern very different from its
predecessor, with a long gallery on the first floor
and rooms for courtiers on the floors above.
Other changes to the palace were superficial.

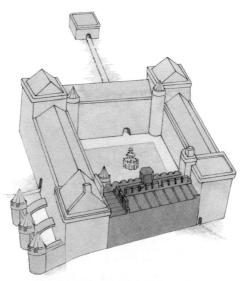

THE COURTYARD: EAST, WEST AND SOUTH FAÇADES

Today, the palace is entered via the arch of James V's south gateway, created around 1535. This leads you into the impressive courtyard, surrounded on all four sides by ranges reflecting the contributions of different monarchs.

The **east side** is the earliest of the four, being essentially James I's design, around 1430. The main entrance to the palace was originally on this side. Directly above it are three niches that once held statues representing the Three Estates (the bishops, nobility and burgesses), although only one pair of feet survives. The stone brackets below are finely carved with figures representing musicians, including one playing the bagpipes (centre). The canopies above represent ornate fairy-tale castles. At the apex, an angel with outstretched wings completes the decoration. All the statues here and elsewhere in the palace were painted in bright colours for James V in 1534.

The door to the left of the entrance, at first-floor level, was inserted at a later date, perhaps by James IV, and became the entrance to the great hall. It originally had a flight of steps leading to it, but these were removed in the 1530s when the doorway was blocked and the space made into a pantry. The blocked doorway was opened up again in the 1800s.

The row of small windows at first-floor level lit a narrow wall passage behind. The larger windows above these were inserted by James IV in the 1490s to improve the great hall's lighting.

Top left: The courtyard façade of the east range, with the north range on the left and the fountain silhouetted in the foreground.

Left: The south-east corner of the courtyard. The turnpikes, or stair-towers, at the corners were installed by James IV.

The **west side** largely reflects the work of James IV in around 1490, and contained the king's lodging, hall and presence chamber on the first floor. Originally, three identical round-headed windows lit the first and second floors, but those on the left were enlarged around 1620 when the north range was rebuilt for James VI. The lower window pediment bears James VI's cipher 'IR6'.

The unusual 14-light 'ladder' window, added by James V in around 1535, once lit an ornate ceiling in the king's presence chamber behind (see page 18). Below this window, a doorway at courtyard level leads into the king's vast wine cellar (see page 23).

The **south side** of the interior façades is largely James IV's, created around 1500. The three tiers of windows, lighting galleries behind, are in the English Perpendicular style and may have been influenced by James's pro-English stance which culminated in his marriage to Margaret Tudor, daughter of Henry VII, in 1503.

The regularity of the windows is broken by the archway of the south entrance. We do not know what statue formerly stood immediately above the arch. However, the statue of the Virgin Mary, and the Pot of Lilies (representing her purity) clearly formed part of an Annunciation scene (the Angel Gabriel announcing Jesus's Incarnation to Mary).

The **turnpike stairs** in all four corners of the courtyard are also James IV's, dating from around 1500.

DID YOU KNOW...

Much of the grey and yellow sandstone from which the palace was built came from quarries at Kingscavil and Fairnie Craig, a couple of miles east of Linlithgow. Although the palace developed over two centuries, stone of a similar colour was used throughout this period. Gormyre, near Torphichen, was the source of the lime used in the construction.

Above: The west range, where James IV installed his king's lodging. The ladder window was added by James V to bring more light into the presence chamber.

Top: The statues above the south entrance represent the Annunciation. The only figures surviving are the Virgin (right) and the Pot of Lilies (centre).

THE COURTYARD: NORTH FAÇADE

The north side of the courtyard is dominated by James VI's range, completed in 1620. The king had long since departed to London to reign as James I of England, but on visiting the palace in 1617 he issued orders for its construction.

James VI's 'new work' replaced the original north range, which had collapsed in 1607. An important clue to the character of the earlier structure can be seen from the courtyard. Midway between the bottom of the central stair and the north-east turnpike stair to its right is the right-hand side of a window that was clearly once large and impressive.

The four tiers of symmetrical pediment windows on the new range are highly reminiscent of Danish court architecture, reminding us that James's wife Queen Anna was the daughter of the king of Denmark.

The subjects of the carvings symbolise the Union of the Crowns in 1603 (when James VI became James I of England also). Look out especially for: IR6 (Jacobus Rex VI) with the Scottish thistle above, IR1 (Jacobus Rex I) with the English rose above, and the initials CP (Carolus Princeps – Prince Charles, the future Charles I) with the Prince of Wales's feathers. There are also *fleurs de lis* (for France) and harps (for Ireland). Also represented are the Honours of Scotland (the crown, sceptre and sword).

In 1629, the turnpike stair in the south-west corner was known as the 'king's turnpike' – it was given special emphasis by the ogee-shaped lintel above the entrance and the large statue (now gone) that stood over it. The stair in the north-west corner was the 'queen's turnpike' – it had a slightly smaller statue above its entrance, also gone. The stair in the north-east corner was the 'kitchen turnpike' (though, being built of rubble rather than ashlar, it may not be of the same date as the other three); the fourth, in the south-east corner, was not named.

Above: The courtyard façade of the north range, viewed from the south entrance. It replaced an earlier north range, built around 1500, which collapsed in 1607.

Left: One of the decorated pediments above the north range windows, most of which celebrate King James VI (Jacobus Rex 6). This one has a thistle and a rose, representing Scotland and England.

THE FOUNTAIN

In the centre of the courtyard is the magnificent fountain, created by James V around 1538. It is still functional and is operated at certain times – ask site staff for details.

The fountain is not only decorative, but also declares James's power and sophistication. The tiered arrangement of three basins is surmounted by a crown, representing the king's superiority. Water, symbolising the benefits of his rule, pours from the mouth of the sun-face on the underside of the crown. From here it flows into the topmost basin, and then spouts through the mouths of grotesque human and animal heads into the octagonal trough below. This is decorated with sculpted figures, including a drummer (symbolising music), a man holding a scroll (literature or scripture), and a mermaid (eloquence). These figures conveyed James's status as a patron of the arts. From here, the water flows through the mouths of angels and human figures into the lower trough, embellished with heraldic motifs. Look out for two unicorns (supporters of the Royal Arms), a lion (representing the king), and a winged deer supporting the joined arms of Scotland and France. This refers to the marriage of James to Madeleine de Valois, daughter of King Francis I.

Above: An artist's impression of the fountain as it may have looked when fully painted in James V's time.

After exploring the courtyard, take the 'kitchen turnpike' in the north-east corner of the courtyard, diametrically opposite the stewards' office. This will bring you to the first-floor kitchen.

CONSERVING THE FOUNTAIN

James V's magnificent fountain was probably damaged by the Hanoverian troops who set fire to the palace in 1746. It appears, from illustrations made in the 1840s, that some attempt was made at restoring the structure in the early 1800s. Further work was carried out in the 1930s, including the reconstruction of some of the missing elements in concrete. In 2000, a modern conservation strategy was drawn up, combining the conservation requirements of the masonry with an in-depth understanding of the fountain's significance. Skilled stonemasons replaced the concrete elements in stone, and the conserved and restored fountain was once more unveiled in 2005.

Right: Sculptor Mark Lillywhite at work on the lion during conservation of the fountain in 2004.

JAMES I'S GREAT HALL

The first floor of the palace was known as the '*piano nobile*' (principal floor). The main room in James I's new palace was the great hall, situated above the entrance gateway in the east range. This ranks as one of the finest medieval interiors in Scotland, although its present form reflects its remodelling during the reign of James IV.

Above: An illustration by R.W. Billings of the great hall, around 1850.

In the time of James I, the hall would not have been quite as long, since the flue from the bakehouse beneath once rose up through its north end. The winding mechanism for the drawbridge must also have encroached on the space. Look out for two small, square holes in the outside (east) wall, which are associated with this mechanism; the original main entrance is directly below. From the narrow passage behind the courtyard wall, it is possible to look down into the entrance passage through the portcullis slot.

Above: The great hall as it looks today. The niches between the windows along the east and west walls would have held a variety of statues (see page 42).

Above: The narrow passage along the courtyard side of the great hall at second-floor level.

The great hall must have been a magnificent space in its day, perfect for banquets, sittings of parliament, and a variety of royal entertainments. The hall roof once soared high above. The long side walls were festooned with statues (although only the stone brackets remain) and decorated by tapestries or hangings. At the north end, entered from the kitchen turnpike, is a remnant of a large minstrels' gallery.

At the south end of the hall stands the great fireplace, which has three compartments. It was added during the reign of James IV, in around 1500, and was undoubtedly the finest in Scotland. Braziers must have been used to heat the hall before this time. The tall dais window in the outer (east) wall, to the left of the fireplace, was added at the same time as the fireplace and illuminated the dais, or raised platform, where the king and queen sat. Above them, a great 'cloth of estate', emblazoned with the royal arms – the lion rampant – would have been displayed. This explains the other name for the great hall – the 'lyon chamber'.

In the north-east corner is the court kitchen which served the great hall. The three serving hatches (one now blocked) allowed food to be passed into the hall. Inside the kitchen is a large fireplace, with an oven in the left side and a tiny storage cellar on the right, with a salt box beside the fireplace. This was the domain of the master cook, and the words 'good[?] cooke' with a date, probably 1637, can be made out on the right side of the fireplace arch.

The kitchen as we see it today is clearly a remodelling of the original. The remains of large stone springers in the side walls indicate that this kitchen was once a high room covered by a great stone vault.

Above: The grand fireplace installed by James IV at the south end of the great hall.

Go through the doorway to the left of the great hall fireplace, pause to look at the royal toilet in the wall-closet, and then enter the room beyond, the dais chamber.

THE CHAPEL

The chapel was installed by James IV in the 1490s, in a space which may previously have been royal apartments. Evidence of its role as a place of worship remains in the form of tall windows and delicate stone-carvings.

The room to the south of the great hall was formerly two smaller rooms, as the two fireplaces suggest. The masonry tusking in the wall to the right of the first fireplace, in the south wall, is what remains of the dividing wall. This first room, entered directly off the great hall, was the **dais chamber**, a withdrawing room to which the king and his high-table guests could retire when they had tired of the company in the great hall.

The room to its west was most probably the **priest's chamber**, conveniently located beside the chapel. A flight of steps led down to a strongroom, probably a sacristy and treasury where the priest stored the valuables entrusted to him, including saintly relics and altar plate.

Go through the door to the left of the fireplace in the west wall and cross the narrow corridor into the chapel.

Above: The chapel as it might have looked when completed in the 1490s.

Far left: A cross carved into the wall of the chapel.

Left: One of the carvings of musical angels on the statue niches between the windows.

The **chapel** was built during the reign of James IV, around 1492. Before that time, this part of the palace was clearly living accommodation, probably the original royal lodging for James I, as the remnant of a fireplace in the right corner of the far (west) wall demonstrates. (The latrine chute serving the lodging is visible outside – see page 27.)

An important aspect of medieval kingship was the perception of the sovereign as a ruler designated by God. The new royal chapel was therefore a significant feature of James IV's new palace. However, apart from several consecration crosses incised on the south-facing wall, there is now little to indicate its role as a chapel. The altar was placed against the east wall, adjacent to the priest's chamber beyond; iron pins in that wall probably held the ornate retable – a panel at the back of the altar. Opposite the altar, at the west end, was a timber screen with a loft above.

This was the musicians' gallery, and probably where the Frenchman Gilyem installed an organ in 1513. The musicians entered through the large arched opening in the side wall. You can see beguiling carvings of angel musicians, attired in choristers' robes, carved on the statue niches between the five tall south-facing windows. The sloping sills of the windows have all been removed at some point.

Before leaving this room, look at the small window to the right of the musicians' entrance. You will see that its right side is dressed at an angle to enable those peeping through from the corridor behind to get a good view of the altar. Was this perhaps where the royal toddler princes and princesses were held in their nurses' arms during celebrations of the Mass?

Go through the west door of the chapel and explore the remaining rooms in the south-west corner of the palace, including the upper floors. There is a museum in the corridor alongside the chapel, displaying many objects found in and around the palace. When you have finished exploring, go through into the west range, the king's lodging.

Above: A floor tile on display in the museum. Originally from James IV's presence chamber, it features the entwined initials I and M, for James and Margaret.

Above left: The tall, south-facing windows that lit the chapel.

Top right: Part of a five-pronged spear displayed in the museum. It was probably used to fish for eels in Linlithgow Loch.

JAMES IV'S LODGING: KING'S HALL

The first floor of the west range is occupied by the king's lodging, a suite of rooms completed during the reign of James IV, in around 1500. The arrangement of rooms represents a progression towards privacy typical in royal and noble lodgings of the time.

The rooms comprising James IV's lodging were recorded in an inventory of 1629, drawn up during preparations for the visit of Charles I in 1633. They were then known as the king's hall, presence chamber and bedchamber, though James IV probably knew them as his hall, great chamber and inner chamber. Each room was graded in importance, according to the rank of guest permitted to enter. There was a similar arrangement of rooms directly above on the second floor, which may at some stage have been the queen's apartment.

The largest room on the first floor, and the lowest in status, was the **king's hall**. The large hooded fireplace in the far (north) wall was the main focus of a room that contained few furnishings. Windows offered fine views eastward across the courtyard, and west over the royal gardens to the park and loch beyond. The three small windows in the courtyard wall once lit an ornate ceiling (now vanished). Other lighting around the palace was probably by means of candles. The two aumbries (wall cupboards) would have been used to store valuables. A door in the window bay to the right of the fireplace gives access to a small stair within the wall thickness, leading down to the cellar below.

Above the king's hall was another chamber of equal size, although its fireplace is in the courtyard wall. It also had a high ceiling, as the roof crease in the south wall shows. Turn to page 47 to find out how this room might have been used.

Go through the door to the left of the fireplace. Had you been visiting in James IVs day, you would have had your credentials checked by a court usher positioned at this point.

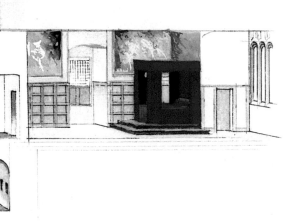

Left: A cutaway illustration showing the three rooms of the king's lodging installed by James IV. The king's hall, on the left, was the most public, while the bedchamber, on the right, was the most private.

JAMES IV'S LODGING: PRESENCE CHAMBER

The second room in the sequence of three was the king's presence chamber. It was smaller in size than the king's hall, but greater in importance.

The presence chamber appears to have functioned as a reception room, where the monarch would receive visitors. It is likely that music was performed and enjoyed in the royal lodging.

The unusual 'ladder' window in the courtyard wall helped cast light onto the ceiling, which would once have been elaborate. Below it, the square aumbry, or wall cupboard, may have displayed the king's finest silver plate.

The fireplace in the opposite wall, with capitals portraying human and lions' heads, is almost identical to ones in James V's palace in Stirling Castle (though the columns are missing). James V added both the fireplace and the ladder window, possibly in preparation for the arrival of Mary of Guise, his second wife, in 1538. Traces of orange, red and black paint, observed on the fireplace in 1860, hint that it was once brightly painted.

Bottom left: James IV's presence chamber. The two large east-facing windows would have been in shade for much of the year, prompting James V to add a ladder window above.

Below right: The west-facing windows allow plenty of afternoon sun into the room. The decorative fireplace was added by James V.

Go through the door to the left of the ladder window and cross the passage into the king's bedchamber.

JAMES IV'S LODGING: BEDCHAMBER

The third room in the sequence was the king's bedchamber, the smallest of the three, but also the most important. Its present appearance belies its former glory, but there are clues that this was once a very special room.

The room had three closets, or side-chambers. In the south-west corner (to the left of the door as you enter) was a closet where the king washed and used the lavatory. Steps in the floor at the entrance to the closet lead down to another closet, the king's strongroom or treasury, where his valuables were securely stored during his stay. (The strongroom is not normally open to visitors for safety reasons.)

The third closet faced north over the loch. This was clearly a fine room, complete with a small fireplace, wood-panelled walls and a vaulted ceiling once brightly painted and still embellished with bosses bearing unicorns. The bosses have little mottoes carved on them – *belle à vous seul* ('beautiful to you alone'), and *jamais ailleurs* ('never elsewhere'). Now sadly missing from this closet is the oriel window that projected out from the north wall.

Fortunately, the oriel window in the neighbouring space does survive. This has been identified as the 'king's oratory', or private chapel, since the high window sill would have provided space for a small altar. Like the neighbouring closet, it has a fireplace, and ceiling bosses displaying unicorns. This oratory was formerly twinned with an oratory for the queen to its east, but this was almost entirely destroyed when the north range collapsed in 1607. Now, only its base survives. You can appreciate these oriels far better from the outside (see page 25).

Above: Inside the oriel window in the king's oratory.

Far left: The vaulted ceiling of the king's oratory.

Left: One of the unicorn ceiling bosses.

QUEEN MARGARET'S BOWER

Towering above the rest of the palace is a small room traditionally associated with Queen Margaret, the English wife of James IV. Little is known about its original function, but it is still the best place from which to admire the view.

At the top of the north-west turnpike stair is a small chamber known as 'Queen Margaret's Bower'. Furnished with wall-seats, it offers extensive views across the surrounding landscape and over the town. Tradition has it that this is where Queen Margaret sat in the autumn of 1513 awaiting in vain her husband's return from waging war on the English at Flodden:

'His own Queen Margaret, who, in Lithgow's bower, All lonely sat, and wept the weary hour.'

(from Sir Walter Scott's *Marmion*)

Left: Queen Margaret, the wife of James IV, forever associated with the room at the top of the queen's turnpike.

A ROYAL NURSERY

The Stewart queens especially appear to have liked Linlithgow's tranquillity and fresh air. Although their lives involved frequent travelling, they made the palace their home as often as they could. It formed part of the marriage dowry of both James III's queen, Margaret of Denmark, and James IV's queen, Margaret Tudor of England.

This fondness of the ladies for the place may account for the birth here of two sovereigns. In April 1512, Queen Margaret Tudor gave birth to her fourth child, Prince James. The little prince's cradle and nurse are both mentioned in the Lord High Treasurer's Accounts. The youngster had barely learned to toddle around the royal apartments when he found himself King James V in September 1513. Thirty years later, James's own queen, Marie, daughter of the duke of Guise-Lorraine, gave birth to their third child, Princess Mary, at Linlithgow Palace on 8 December 1542. She found herself queen just six days later.

Above: Queen Elizabeth of Bohemia, grand-daughter of Mary Queen of Scots, was raised at Linlithgow.

Right: An oak cradle from Linlithgow. Although traditionally associated with Mary, it probably dates from the 1600s.

Another royal toddler brought up in the nursery was Mary's granddaughter, Elizabeth (1596–1662), better known to history as 'the Winter Queen' following her marriage to the king of Bohemia. Lady Livingston, her governess, and Bessie MacDowell and Alison Hay, her two nurses, made great fuss of her, and the Accounts record purchases of a hairbrush and four dolls for the young girl.

THE NORTH RANGE

The north range is almost entirely James VI's, built around 1620. This building replaced an earlier north range, which collapsed in 1607.

James VI's 'new work' as his north range became known, comprised four floors of living accommodation above a storage basement. On the first floor, now accessible via a timber walkway, is the principal room, the long gallery, situated between the royal lodgings in the west range and the kitchens in the east. The two fireplaces were gilded in preparation for Charles I's visit in 1633. The north range has fine windows overlooking the loch, and there is a small toilet closet at the east end of the long gallery.

The remainder of the north range contained rooms for courtiers and officials of the royal household. Altogether, there were 14 two-roomed suites, although the partitions between these have not survived. The chimneys in the north range are particularly numerous since they had to serve a total of 39 fireplaces. By 1648, the earl of Linlithgow, in his capacity as hereditary keeper of the palace, was residing here with his household.

In 1746, a fire started here in the north range, and eventually consumed the whole palace in flames. If you look carefully, you will see charred stumps of floor joists and heat-cracked stones.

Go through the doorway at the far end of the timber walkway. The room beyond is a much-altered space: in 1648 it was divided into two, a private chamber overlooking the loch, and the earl of Linlithgow's pantry, looking onto the courtyard. Cross this room, enter the kitchen turnpike and go down to the very bottom of the stair.

Above left: A row of chimneys at the top of the north range, which had 39 fireplaces.

Above: The long gallery as it may have looked on completion in 1620. The elegant decorative scheme was obliterated in the fire of 1746.

THE GROUND FLOOR AND CELLARS

The ground and below-ground floors were used for storage and for the palace's administrative functions. The specific roles played by a few rooms are still known.

The room at the foot of the kitchen turnpike is the laich (or lower) kitchen. This complemented the court kitchen (see page 13) in providing food for banquets in the great hall. The large fireplace here was wide enough to accommodate a small boy, known as a 'turnbrochie', whose task was to turn the spits of roasting meat.

Other servants included the 'groom of the kitchen door', the 'yeomen of the great and petty larders' and the 'pateser', or pastry-cook. The square recesses around the walls are aumbries, or wall cupboards, where spices and other items where stored.

The laich kitchen was originally designed in the 1430s as the 'well chamber', and the draw-well, 9m deep, still survives. The palace staff also drew water from the trough next to the courtyard fountain. Adjacent to the kitchen are cellars used for storing food.

Make your way back up to the courtyard and into the original entrance passage in the east range. Look out for the portcullis slot, three sets of gates, the slots for the drawbridge, and an arched recess in the right-hand wall where the porters could stand while a large cart entered. Go through the door to the right of that recess into the guardroom and prison.

Top right: Steps leading down to the wine cellar in the west range.

Right: The large fireplace and well in the laich, or lower kitchen.

Above: A comical carved figure in the wine cellar, outlined in white for added clarity.

The **guardroom** was used by the porters, or guards, who controlled access into James I's palace. The porters slept here, and used the latrine closet at the back of the room. Their duties included patrolling the premises, operating the drawbridge and portcullis, and ringing the palace bell (located on the battlements) to keep everyone to time.

They were also required to guard prisoners in the underground cell. These were brought into the guardroom and lowered through the hatch in the recess to the left of the entrance door, into the prison. This grim space (not normally open to visitors for safety reasons), lies below the entrance passage. It includes a latrine but there is no window to offer light and fresh air.

Return to the courtyard and turn left to view the cellars in the south-east corner. Next visit the wine cellar in the west range. It is entered though the door below the ladder window.

The **wine cellar**, built for James IV in around 1495, is split into two rooms. The lower one incorporates a fine stone-vaulted ceiling. The corbels supporting this are carved with amusing figures drinking from flagons. The vast scale of the wine cellar offers a clue to the large number of people residing in the palace when their majesties were in residence, and of the scale of the banquets in the great hall.

That completes the guided tour of the palace interior. Now exit the palace via James V's main south entrance and turn right to examine the exterior.

EXTERIOR: WEST AND NORTH FRONTS

The layout of the palace changed repeatedly throughout its development, and these changes are of course reflected in the exterior. The north range was rebuilt as recently as 1620, but the structure has changed little since then.

The **west front** (to your left as you face the main entrance) holds important clues as to how the palace came to be the shape it is. Of course, none of those clues would have been seen by visitors to the royal court, for all the walls would have been rendered (that is, covered) with a coat of lime harl.

On the far right, just left of the lightning conductor, there is a vertical joint running up the full height of the south-west tower. The masonry to the left of this joint is James III's, built around the 1470s, and marks his contribution to the palace – an L-shaped royal lodging forming the south-west corner of the palace quadrangle. His son, James IV, later incorporated this into his own more elaborate royal lodging along this west range.

The masonry to the right of this joint belongs to James V's scheme to form a second entrance into the palace from the south. This involved 'ironing out' a kink in the south wall, caused when James III added his royal lodging onto that built by his grandfather, James I, in the 1420s.

Scars in the masonry, midway along the west front, offer a clue to the former existence of a projecting stone feature, entered through two doors (now blocked) in the king's lodging. This may have been a latrine block, or perhaps more likely a balcony giving views over the formal gardens that would have been laid out on this side of the palace.

Above: The west front.

Above: The north front.

The **north front** is mostly James VI's, built around 1620. He installed the windows with the stone dividers (the verticals are called mullions and the horizontals transoms), and almost all were of that form. However, the projecting oriel windows at the lower right-hand side are earlier. Enough survives to show that there were originally three oriels (an arrangement mirrored at the royal lodging in Edinburgh Castle). The one remaining largely intact lit the 'king's oratory' (see page 19), and its neighbour, to its left, was the 'queen's oratory' (only the base of which survives). Between these two oriels, at ground level, is the postern, or back door, perhaps used by servants entering and leaving their workplace.

Above: The oriel window of the king's oratory with the postern below.

EXTERIOR: EAST AND SOUTH FRONTS

Above: The east front, with the original entrance to the palace. The barbican, right of
the entrance, was added by James IV to improve the defences and support the structure.

The east range dates back to the earliest days of the palace, built by James I.
The projecting barbican to the right of the entrance was added by James IV,
to enhance its appearance, strengthen the defences and bolster the structure.

The **east front** is not only the oldest but also the most attractive. This is because it was
the entrance front, or 'fore-face', for much of the palace's life. At its centre stands James I's
triumphant entrance gate, built around 1430 (see illustration, page 39).

The tall canopied niches on either side of the entrance once held statues, perhaps of
St Andrew (Scotland's patron saint) and St James (the king's namesake). Above the gate,
a rectangular panel displays the royal arms (the lion rampant) on a shield, flanked by a
pair of angels. Another angel with outstretched wings completes the composition
(see illustration, page 39).

The two long, vertical slots held the gaffs, the beams from which the drawbridge was
suspended. The drawbridge itself and the outer ramp that led up to it are both long gone.
The other significant feature on this east side is the remnant of the 'utter grete bulwark',
a barbican, or forework, added by James IV around 1495, perhaps for defensive reasons,
but more likely to add an impression of castellated grandeur to an otherwise non-
fortified palace. The flying buttresses, highly visible today but once hidden behind
the forework's towers, acted as structural props at this weakest corner of the palace.

Far left: The south front, which includes the south entrance, added by James V in the 1530s.

Left: The tall windows of the chapel installed by James IV are a feature of the south front.

The **south front** became the palace's entrance façade during the time of James V, probably around 1535. The projecting gateway is flanked by small, circular towers, incorporating oval gunloops. The five tall windows on the first floor, to the right of the gate, date from around 1492 and lit the chapel behind. Beneath them, at ground level, the arched opening represents a latrine cesspit, indicating that before the chapel was built this part of the palace served as the royal lodging.

Finally, the wall to the left of the entrance is pockmarked with round holes, said to have been made by Cromwell's soldiers firing their muskets.

That concludes the guided tour of the palace. As you leave, take time to visit the 15th-century St Michael's Church, which still serves as the parish church.

THE OUTER GATEWAY

The outer gateway or 'fore entrance' was built for James V around 1535, and gave access to the peel, or outer enclosure, surrounding the palace. It represented the point at which the visitor passed from the ordinary, everyday world into the elevated environment of the Stewart royal court. The four panels above the arch proclaim the status of the sovereign residing within. They signify that King James V was a member of four orders of chivalry: the Garter of England, the Thistle of Scotland, the Golden Fleece of Burgundy and St Michael of France. The original panels were replaced by replicas in the 19th century.

THE PEEL AND LOCH

The peel, or royal park, surrounds the palace and provides an attractive setting for what is arguably the most impressive of Scotland's medieval palaces.

From the beginning, the peel formed an integral part of the royal residence. The space was used in a variety of ways, as gardens and orchards, and for sporting activities such as archery, tennis and jousting. It is likely that several ancillary buildings, largely of timber, were constructed on the peel, perhaps including workshops and stables for horses.

The palace was built on a promontory that slopes steeply down to the loch on the west. On the east side there is a large expanse of level parkland that may, at least in part, have been reclaimed from formerly marshy ground. The land immediately around the palace has been terraced, possibly during the 1500s.

Top: A view of the palace and peel from the north side of the loch by M. Bouquet, dated 1849.

Above: An aerial view from the north-east shows the contours of the peel.

Recent archaeological survey and excavation work in the peel has added weight to the possibility of prehistoric or Roman occupation of the promontory. Fragments of Roman pottery have been found in the peel over the years.

The loch appears to contain the remains of two crannogs. In addition, the loch shores have seen extensive use, not just by the palace but also by the town. Several industries were reliant on the loch, including tanning and glue-making. The loch was an important source of food for the palace, providing swans, ducks, eels and fish.

Nowadays, the peel and loch are protected as a Scheduled Ancient Monument and a Site of Special Scientific Interest. The peel offers attractive open space for townspeople and visitors alike to enjoy, and together with the loch supports a variety of recreational activities.

DID YOU KNOW . . .

Linlithgow's coat of arms features a black dog apparently tethered to an oak tree. There is an associated local legend, of a black greyhound whose master was sentenced to starve to death on an island in the loch. The dog would swim from the town every day with food for him and was thus able to save his life. Whether or not there is any truth to this story, the town's residents adopted the dog as their symbol, and are sometimes referred to as 'black bitches'.

CRANNOGS IN THE LOCH

Recent archaeological survey work suggests that two of the small, tree-covered islands in Linlithgow Loch represent the remains of crannogs. A crannog is a type of loch dwelling, consisting of an artificial or modified natural island, built to accommodate an individual home or an extended family, and often connected to the shore by a timber causeway. Some may have been used as fishing or hunting bases. The oldest-known crannogs probably date from the Neolithic period, 5,000 years ago. Documentary sources reveal that some Scottish crannogs were still in use as late as the 1600s. Today, the two examples in the loch are home to the nests of ducks and other birds.

Right: One of the crannogs on Linlithgow Loch as it may have looked when in use.

LOCH LIFE

Linlithgow Loch is the largest body of fresh water in the Lothian area. It has many interesting and important wildlife habitats, including open water, water plants, emergent vegetation, grassland and woodland. The water plants are of particular interest, and as a result the loch is protected by its status as a Site of Special Scientific Interest.

The loch was formed during the latter part of the last Ice Age. As the glaciers retreated, a large broken block of ice was left in the landscape. As it melted, the resulting sediment built up around it, leaving a water-filled depression.

Many animals depend on the loch, notably Daubenton's bats, which live in nearby buildings and trees. At night they feed low over the water, hunting for the many insects found flying above the loch. Linlithgow Palace is an important nursery roost site where the female Daubentons raise their young. During the day in summer swallows, house martins, sand martins and swifts are frequently seen over the loch, feeding on the myriad insects emerging from the water. Linlithgow still has a good number of swift nests within the town's houses. Otters have been known to frequent the loch and its associated burns, and water shrews are occasionally seen.

The loch is of particular interest for water birds, especially the resident populations of great crested grebe and mute swans. The usual three breeding pairs of great crested grebes are a significant proportion of the Lothian total, while the loch generally has the largest inland population of mute swans in the Lothian region, with the permanent population bolstered by winter incomers. Little grebe also breed on the loch, while the autumn moult flock has been recorded at over fifty birds.

There are also large flocks of other waterfowl, mainly mallard, coot, pochard, golden eye and the largest population of tufted duck in the Lothians. The mallard, coot and some of the tufted duck remain over the summer, while the pochard and golden eye are winter visitors, along with a flock of greylag geese. Feeding the birds is a popular pastime, but overfeeding causes problems for the loch, increasing nutrient levels and causing harmful algal blooms. If you want to feed the birds, please use no more than two slices of wholemeal bread or a handful of grain.

The water plants are essential to life within the loch. Submerged plants grow in the shallows, most commonly fennel or sago pondweed. The sago pondweed is especially important food for waterfowl as the tubers are high in starch. The emergent stems of other plants such as reedmace provide places on which dragonflies and damselflies can land. Their larvae crawl on the stems during their transformation into adults. The plant's leaves and roots also provide shade and shelter for many other small aquatic invertebrates. They are also invaluable nesting sites for waterbirds, providing food and cover from predators.

This page: Swans, geese, coots, ducks and other water birds on the loch in winter.

THE HISTORY OF
LINLITHGOW
PALACE

A castle or manor existed at Linlithgow at the time of David I, the founder of the burgh, who reigned 1124–53. Edward I of England exploited the potential of the site as a military base in the early 1300s and created a garrison fortress.

After the Wars of Independence, the old castle was restored for royal use once more, but a great fire in 1424 destroyed the castle and much of the town. From the ashes rose James I's new 'pleasure palace', where the sovereigns of the royal house of Stewart held court in grand style.

The following pages tell the story of Linlithgow Palace, its triumphs and tragedies, from its origins in the 12th century to its demise six centuries later.

THE LOCH IN THE DAMP HOLLOW

The name Linlithgow means 'the loch in the damp hollow' – a compound of *llyn* 'loch', *llaith* 'damp' and *cau* 'hollow' (as in the name Glasgow 'the green hollow'). The palace stands on a promontory overlooking the small loch.

Robert Burns, Scotland's national poet, described Linlithgow Palace as 'sweetly situated'. Historically, its location was both attractive and easily defensible. Finds of Roman pottery and recent archaeological survey work have indicated the possibility that there was some prehistoric or Roman settlement in the area, and two possible crannogs (see page 29) have recently been identified in the loch.

Above: An engraving of the peel and palace by James Collie, dating from the 1850s.

Above: Holyrood Abbey in Edinburgh, whose canons received skins from Linlithgow's cattle and sheep in 1143.

Left: David I, based on an illustration from a medieval manuscript.

We know that David I had a castle at Linlithgow by 1143. In that year, he granted skins from the cattle and sheep pastured there to the canons of Holyrood Abbey in Edinburgh. By then, a town and church had grown up under the castle's protection. King David's heirs, Malcolm IV (1153–65) and William I (1165–1214), both sealed charters at Linlithgow Castle.

No trace has ever been found of this first royal residence, but a reference by the bishop of Liège to the 'mansum de Linlithcu' in a 13th-century document suggests a lightly defended manor house rather than a formidable castle. All this changed, however, with the appearance of Edward I of England's invasion army in the summer of 1296.

TIMELINE

1143	AROUND 1190

DAVID I
grants the Augustinian canons of Holyrood Abbey animal skins from Linlithgow – the earliest record of royal occupation.

WILLIAM I 'THE LION'
seals a charter at Linlithgow Castle, a further indication that it had become a royal settlement.

EDWARD I'S PEEL

Above: Edward I of England, who chose Linlithgow as one of his military strongholds during his attempted conquest of Scotland in the early 1300s. This statue stands at Lincoln Cathedral.

In 1296, Edward I of England led an invasion of Scotland. This marked the beginning of the Wars of Independence, a 60-year period of conflict which devastated much of the country. During this time, Edward and his successors took up temporary residence at various Scottish castles.

Edward I did not reside at Linlithgow Castle in 1296. However, he did camp on the Burgh Muir, to the east of Linlithgow, before the Battle of Falkirk in 1298, at which he defeated William Wallace. When he returned to Scotland in 1301, the 'king's chamber' in Linlithgow Castle was prepared for him.

Edward saw Linlithgow's potential as a military base, and gave instructions for converting the castle into a secure stronghold, as a base from which to attack Stirling Castle. He employed his finest brains, most crucially Master James of St George, architect of the great castles of North Wales that had helped secure Edward's conquest of that land.

Edward's Linlithgow base was built almost entirely in timber, probably because stone would have been too expensive. Throughout 1302–3, Master James's huge team of carpenters, masons and quarriers toiled to create the garrison fortress. They isolated the castle and church from the town by digging a great ditch across the promontory. Behind this they erected a 'pele' – a stockade of split tree trunks (from the Old French *pel*, meaning 'stake'). This is the origin of the name Linlithgow Peel, now applied to the park surrounding the palace.

Midway along the pele, Master James built a defended gatehouse, and at either end a wooden tower rising up from the waters of the loch. Inside, the church was strengthened and converted into a storehouse. Finally, a second ditch and stockade were built around the promontory to defend the castle against attack from the loch. This work was finished by the end of 1303, and used by Edward in 1304 for his assault on Stirling. At one point, 21 wagon-loads of timber, lead and stone ammunition were dispatched from Linlithgow to the English camp there.

Left: Drawn in 1678 by the military draughtsman John Slezer, the palace still looks well defended.

Linlithgow Peel remained in English hands for the next decade, a useful supply base along the route between Stirling and Edinburgh. Edward's son and successor Edward II spent a week there in October 1310. In the end, though, the garrison could not hold out against the growing Scottish resistance under King Robert the Bruce. It was retaken in 1313, and Bruce's biographer, John Barbour, gives a wonderful poetic account of its capture, with a local farmer, William Bunnock, cast as unlikely hero:

'In the country there dwelt one who was a husbandman. And by his cattle often led hay to the peel. He was called William Bunnock, and was a stalwart man in a fight … He got men who could make an ambush, while he went with his cart to the peel … The porter, who saw him clearly coming near the gate, opened it soon, when Bunnock, without hesitation, had the cart move straight on. And when it was set evenly between the door-checks of the gate, so that no-one could get by, he shouted 'call all, call all', and then he [the yeoman leading the ox] let the goad drop, and quickly cut the cart ropes in two. Bunnock, with that, struck the porter such a blow that blood and brains both were spilled. And those who were inside the cart jumped out with agility and soon killed the men of the castle who were near. Then for a while there was shouting; those lying in ambush nearby leapt out, came with drawn swords and took all the castle, without trouble, and slew those who were inside … In this way Bunnock with his wain took the peel … then gave it to the king who rewarded him worthily and had it knocked down to the ground.'

Nothing remains now of Edward's peel. But walking around the promontory, the visitor will not find it hard to imagine the vast military entrenchment that once enclosed it.

1298

WILLIAM WALLACE is defeated by Edward I at the Battle of Falkirk, 8 miles (13km) west of Linlithgow.

1310

EDWARD II OF ENGLAND spends a week at Linlithgow Peel during a 12-year English occupation.

THE FIRE AND THE NEW PALACE

After the Wars of Independence, Linlithgow Castle became a royal residence. However, it was not until after it was destroyed by fire that the palace began to take shape.

Linlithgow was restored to royal use in 1337 on the orders of David II. He took up residence in the castle, and held court here in 1343. Shortly after his death in 1371, Scotland's Parliament, the Three Estates, met at Linlithgow to elect a new king. They chose Bruce's grandson Sir Robert Stewart, who became Robert II, the first in a long succession of Stewart monarchs. Although he and his son Robert III (1390–1406) spent much of the time in their native west of Scotland, they did authorise repairs to the king's 'house' or 'manor' at Linlithgow for their occasional visits.

In 1424, a disastrous fire swept through the town of Linlithgow. Both the castle and church were caught in the conflagration. James I (1406–37) had only recently returned from lengthy captivity in England – and turned tragedy into triumph. Determined to reassert royal authority after years of ineffectual royal rule, James ordered a new royal palace be built over the ashes of the old one.

James's prime aim was to emphasise the cult of kingship by building a 'pleasure palace' that would leave his subjects gazing open-mouthed in admiration. It would be a statement in stone that this king was on a far loftier plane than his nobles. As a prisoner in England, James had witnessed at first hand how his English counterparts, Henry IV and Henry V, had used building works to command respect from their subjects.

Top left: David II, who restored Linlithgow to royal use in 1337.

Left: Coins showing the heads of the first two kings of the Stewart succession, Robert II (left) and Robert III. Although they rarely visited Linlithgow, both authorised repairs to the old castle.

Above: James I, who began a new palace in the 1420s, after the town had been devastated by fire.

The new palace was begun in 1425. By 1429, sufficient progress had been made to enable James to entertain the archbishop of Reims here upon his arrival from France. By now the word 'palace' had replaced both 'castle' and 'peel'. In 1434, payments to Matthew, the king's painter, hint that the sculpture, ceilings and wall-plaster were being decorated according to the fashions of the day. By the time of James's death in 1437, £7,000 had been spent on the works, a huge sum at that time, representing one tenth of the king's income. The building works came to an abrupt halt with James's death.

James II (1437–60) was only seven years old when James I was assassinated in Perth and he became king. There is no record suggesting he took an interest in his father's palace at Linlithgow until 1446. Even then, he seems to have regarded it as a home for his cherished guns rather than his beloved family. The great siege cannon he used to bring down the Black Douglases at Threave Castle in 1455 was kept in the palace.

James III (1460–88) was barely eight when he inherited the throne, but he continued his grandfather's work. In the early 1480s, there are references to the grazing of the palace meadows by horses employed in construction work. There is also clear evidence in the fabric that the move to create a fully enclosed courtyard palace was made in James III's reign. However, it was left to his son, James IV, to complete the pleasure palace envisaged by their ancestor James I.

Above: The east entrance as it may have looked in the 1430s.

1424

A GREAT FIRE destroys much if not all of the old castle. Soon afterwards, James I embarks on building his new palace.

EARLY 1480s

JAMES III advances his grandfather's development of the palace, enlarging the royal lodgings and adding the SW tower.

THEIR MAJESTIES' PALACE

Above: James IV, who developed much of Linlithgow Palace as we see it today.

James IV succeeded his father in 1488. He took a keen interest in Linlithgow Palace, installing his own suite of rooms along the west range, adding the north range and completing the fully enclosed quadrangle.

James IV was a prolific royal builder. From the first year of his reign until his untimely death in 1513, he was engaged in adding to his royal residences. He transformed the medieval castles at Stirling and Falkland into glittering Renaissance palaces, created a new palace out of the ageing monastic guesthouse at Holyrood, erected a splendid new great hall at Edinburgh Castle, and also ordered significant works at lesser royal centres such as Rothesay Castle, on Bute. The royal palace at Linlithgow was no exception.

In the first year of James's reign, the Lord High Treasurer's Accounts record five shillings being spent to send a carpenter from Dundee to inspect the palace work at Linlithgow. From this it appears that construction was already in progress. From the recorded works that followed, it becomes clear that the young king was determined to transform Linlithgow Palace into a modern royal residence. We know a few of the tradesmen's names: Nicholas Jackson and Stephen Balty (Bawty), leading masons; Thomas Pebles, glazier of the great hall windows in 1512; and a Frenchman called Gilyem, who installed the chapel organ in the year the king died.

The work was largely finished by 1503, in time for James's marriage to Margaret Tudor, daughter of Henry VII of England. James presented the palace to his bride as a wedding gift. Scotland and England were also celebrating the sealing of a 'Treaty of Perpetual Peace', stating that there should be 'a true, sincere, whole and unbroken peace, friendship, league and amity … from this day forth in all times to come' between the two nations.

Ten years later, joy turned to sorrow, when King James was killed at Flodden in Northumberland. Tradition has it that Queen Margaret vainly awaited her husband's return in the small chamber at the top of the north-west turnpike stair. The following year, the dowager-queen was forced to flee Scotland, and the palace, recently so busy, fell silent.

Top left: The south-east turnpike and south range. James IV remodelled the south range, inserting windows in the English Perpendicular style.

Above: The west range, also developed by James IV, though his son James V installed the ladder window.

Above left: A detail of the vast fireplace James IV added to the great hall built by his great-grandfather James I.

Above: Inside one of the turnpike stairs, added by James IV around 1500 at the four corners of the courtyard.

1503

MARGARET TUDOR
marries James IV,
who gives her
Linlithgow Palace as
a wedding present.

1513

**THE BATTLE
OF FLODDEN**
sweeps away 8,000
Scottish lives, including
that of James IV.

LIFE AT COURT

Linlithgow Palace was much more than an occasional residence where the king and queen stayed as they travelled along the road between Edinburgh and Stirling. It was an important centre in its own right, where the royal family could see, and be seen by, their subjects.

To an extent, Linlithgow, like Falkland Palace across the Forth in Fife, was seen by its royal owners more as a retreat than a main seat, sufficiently distant from the political cauldrons of Edinburgh and Stirling to enable them to relax. Linlithgow was also considered a healthier environment. In 1585, James VI moved here from Edinburgh because Linlithgow was 'clere and void of all suspitioun of the said seikness [plague]'.

The Stewarts loved Linlithgow. They could enjoy themselves here, feasting in the monumental splendour of the great hall, granting audiences in their sumptuous private apartments, strolling in the pleasure gardens, bowling on the lawns, playing 'catchpule' in the tennis court, practising archery at the shooting butts, hawking in the park, and of course boating on the loch.

The treasurer's accounts are full of fascinating glimpses into life at court around this time. Carriages and carts constantly come and go, bearing the royal family together with their household, furniture, furnishings and baggage. There are references to the king's bed, velvet chairs, tapestries, relics and furniture for the chapels, even the royal dogs. During their stay they are waited on, and entertained, by all manner of attendants, among them a French leech-doctor! Gardeners are paid for seeds and flowers, a beekeeper for bees, and the loch is well stocked with pike, perch and eel.

Top: A carved figure in late-medieval courtly dress, probably part of the decorative scheme of the original palace and now displayed in the museum.

Right: A banquet in the great hall as it may have looked in the days of James IV.

When the royal family was in residence, the people of Linlithgow were kept busy providing the palace with a great variety of goods and services, including food and ceramic vessels for the table, rushes for the chambers, horses, harnesses and hay. Documentary sources tell of a skinner making hawking gloves, and a tailor providing shirts, for their king, and local women brewing ale for the huge royal household. A man named Thomas Kellis supplied new tennis balls for the use of Queen Mary's husband Lord Darnley.

Aristocratic houses were built in the town, including embassies for the kings of France and Spain. The town council celebrated their prosperity by rebuilding St Michael's Church adjacent to the palace, which had been partially destroyed in the 1424 fire. It is likely that many of the craftsmen employed at the palace also worked on the church. They included John and Thomas French, father and son, master masons for James III, James IV and James V. On his death in 1489, John French was laid to rest in the north transept of the church he helped to rebuild.

Top right: The imposing east façade of the palace, with the original main entrance at its centre and James IV's barbican on the right.

Right: A carved figure on St Michael's Church, neighbouring the palace. It was slowly rebuilt after the fire of 1424 by many of the tradesmen who built the palace itself.

DID YOU KNOW . . .

Personal servants of the royal family slept close to their master or mistress. Documentary sources refer to six 'grooms' (young boys) sleeping on canvas beds in the king's bedchamber. Other staff probably bedded down on floors in warm spaces, such as the great hall, the kitchens and the bakehouse.

1528

JAMES V begins his personal reign and soon begins remodelling Linlithgow Palace to display his refined Renaissance tastes.

1539

SIR JAMES HAMILTON OF FINNART is appointed the king's master of works, having been keeper of Linlithgow Palace since 1526. He masterminds major works at several royal palaces.

THE MOST PRINCELY HOME

Like many of his ancestors, James V inherited the throne as a child. During his minority, various regents ruled Scotland, and Linlithgow Palace seems to have stood largely empty and disused. But soon after beginning his personal reign, James V turned his attention to the neglected palace.

In 1528, James V reached the age of 16 and finally freed himself from the control of regents. Before long, he had summoned builders to remodel and refurbish Linlithgow Palace. His contributions were largely embellishments – and he became well-known for such works. He also embellished his castle at Stirling and the royal palaces at Holyrood and Falkland with the very latest Continental architectural fashions.

Above: A figure depicted on James V's fountain, probably symbolising literature or scripture.

Top: Building works in the era of James V. His projects included installing the south entrance and outer gate, and enlarging the south-west tower. St Michael's Church, shown here during its reconstruction, was completed in 1540.

A leading light in the remodelling of Linlithgow Palace was Sir James Hamilton of Finnart, an illegitimate son of the 1st Earl of Arran and a kinsman of James V. Appointed keeper of the palace and park at Linlithgow in 1526, he subsequently rose to become his king's master of works. He had spent several years in mainland Europe gaining knowledge of architecture and fortification, two subjects well-expressed in his new south-facing gateways.

The master mason most closely associated with the works was Thomas French. He was at Linlithgow soon after 1530, putting the finishing touches to his father's church as well as beginning to realise James V's new vision for the palace. He later worked at Falkland Palace, where he was assisted by masons specially brought over from France.

The detailed building accounts kept by Sir James Hamilton and Sir Thomas Johnston, the king's chaplain, provide vivid details of the works being carried out in these years. The main entrance to the palace, on the east side, was moved to the south, and an outer gateway was built to the south of it, giving access to the outer enclosure from the town. The proportions of the south front were also improved by straightening out the south wall and enlarging the south-west tower to

Above: A double portrait of James V and his second wife Mary of Guise.

balance the one on the south-east. In the chapel, a new wooden ceiling and canopied altarpiece were inserted. The great hall was refurnished and provided with new windows, and alterations were also made to the kitchen. Another conspicuous addition was the fountain in the courtyard, said to have run with red wine on special occasions.

James V's contribution to the palace may have been less sweeping in its approach but his embellishments, the fountain in particular, mark an interesting point in the adoption of Renaissance classicism in Scotland. They appear to have had the desired effect. James's queen, Mary of Guise, declared Linlithgow to be a 'very fair palace', as fine as any château in France.

1540

SIR DAVID LYNDSAY OF THE MOUNT
presents his famous morality play *Ane Pleasant Satyre of the Thrie Estaitis* at Linlithgow Palace – this may be its earliest performance.

AROUND 1540

MARY OF GUISE
the second French wife of James V, declares this 'most princely home' as fine as any château in her homeland.

MARY QUEEN OF SCOTS

Left: Mary Queen of Scots, who was born at Linlithgow Palace but was taken to Stirling while still an infant.

Of all the Stewart monarchs, Mary (1542–67) is undoubtedly the one most closely associated with Linlithgow Palace. Yet apart from being born here, on 8 December 1542, she had very little impact on the place.

Mary remained at Linlithgow for just seven months. In July 1543, agreement was reached with England for her marriage to Edward, Prince of Wales. Her mother, Mary of Guise, widow of James V, feared that the infant queen might be abducted in preparation for her eventual marriage. She therefore moved her daughter to the greater safety of Stirling Castle.

Mary did not return to Linlithgow for another 20 years. Even then, it was for only very short stays, although the palace and its surrounding park and garden appear to have been kept in reasonable repair. She last slept at the palace on 23 April 1567. The next day, she rode off towards Edinburgh, only to be intercepted at the Briggs of Almond by her lover, Bothwell, and abducted. Within two months, she was a prisoner at Lochleven Castle.

WHERE WAS MARY BORN?

A question that has exercised many minds over the years is: where was Mary Queen of Scots born – and her father, James V, for that matter? One thing is fairly certain; both births would have taken place in the queen's bedchamber. But where exactly was that? There are three possibilities.

The first possibility is the room directly above the king's bedchamber in the north-west corner (**1**). In its favour is the fact that the second floor of the west range has an almost identical suite of rooms – hall, presence chamber and bedchamber – to the floor below, which was the king's lodging. Logic suggests that this upper floor was therefore the queen's lodging.

However, the room directly above the king's bedchamber is small and has just one north-facing window, and it seems doubtful that this room alone would have been suitable as a bedchamber for successive queens. For the lodging to have functioned to the satisfaction of its royal occupant, both upper floors in the north-west tower may have been needed. This is certainly possible. The adjacent turnpike stair is known as the 'queen's turnpike', and at the very top of the tower is Queen Margaret's Bower. This would mean that James and Mary were born not in the room directly above the king's bedchamber, but in the room above that, on the third floor (**2**).

The third possibility – and perhaps the most likely – is that the queen's lodging was in the earlier north range, the building that collapsed in 1607. The fragments of surviving evidence indicate a grand structure. James and Mary may well have been born in a room immediately to the east of the queen's oratory (**3**) – a room that was part of the earlier north range and has since been replaced.

Above: Queens would have given birth in their bedchamber, located somewhere in the north-west corner of the palace.

1542

MARY QUEEN OF SCOTS
is born at Linlithgow Palace, on 8 December.

1542

JAMES V
dies at Falkland Palace, Fife, on 14 December, and is succeeded by his six-day-old daughter Mary.

A PALACE IN DECLINE

Left: James VI, who spent time at Linlithgow Palace during his personal reign in Scotland (1583–1603). By this time the castle was in a poor state of repair.

In 1567, Mary was forced to abdicate in favour of her infant son, James VI. Scotland was ruled once more by a succession of regents, and Linlithgow Palace was again left neglected.

The regents who governed Scotland during James VI's minority did not stay in the palace. When visiting Linlithgow, they preferred to reside in lodgings in the town. However, this proved to be unwise. In January 1570, while staying in an inn owned by the provost of Linlithgow (on the site now occupied by 117–21 High Street), Regent Moray was murdered by a sniper.

On beginning his personal reign in 1583, James VI used Linlithgow Palace a little more frequently than his mother had done. By then, though, the palace was showing its age. In 1583, Sir Robert Drummond, King James's master of works, reported that the west range of the palace was 'altogidder lyk to fall down'. His warning went unheeded. Parliament met at the palace in 1585, and in 1590 James came here to spend some time with his new bride, Queen Anna, daughter of the king of Denmark. But decay was setting in.

In 1599, an English agent, George Nicholson, observed that 'there is a quarter ruinous and the rest necessary to be repaired'. Four years later, James VI left Scotland for London and the throne of England, leaving his dangerously neglected palace at Linlithgow behind. In 1607, part of the palace came crashing to the ground. Alexander Livingston, the keeper, wrote to James thus: 'This sext of September, betwixt thre and four in the morning, the north quarter of your Majesties Palace of Linlythgw is fallin, rufe and all, within the wallis, to the ground; but the wallis ar standing yit, bot lukis everie moment when the inner wall sall fall, and brek your Majesty's fontan.'

Livingston added that he would have been to blame had he not informed the king about the state of the palace two years earlier. It would be another 11 years before work on the new north range was begun.

Above: The pediment on the central window of the west range is carved in honour of James VI. This carving was part of the building scheme after the collapse of the north range in 1607.

1570

REGENT MORAY is assassinated at his lodgings in Linlithgow on 23 January.

1590

ANNA OF DENMARK spends time at Linlithgow Palace with her new husband James VI.

ROYAL WITHDRAWAL

The story of Linlithgow Palace as a royal residence might have ended with the departure of the Stewart court for London in 1603 and the collapse of the north range a few years after. But James VI did return to Scotland – just once, in 1617. In the euphoria surrounding his brief visit to Linlithgow, he issued instructions that the north range be rebuilt.

The new north range was built under the direction of the master mason William Wallace, and represents, even now, one of the finest Renaissance façades in Scotland. The work began in 1618 and took six years to complete. The symmetrical arrangement of the exterior was mirrored in the planning of the interior. In keeping with the finest fashion of the day, the first floor contained a new long gallery, on the side overlooking the loch. King James, however, never returned to see his resurrected palace.

His son, Charles I (1625–49) was born in Scotland, but did not visit his homeland until 1633. A small fortune was spent preparing the palace for his visit to Linlithgow. The hereditary keeper, the earl of Linlithgow, had to move himself, his family and belongings out of the north range – and the jackdaws were evicted from the chimneys. Windows and doors were renewed, and the stables rebuilt.

Preparations were also made in the town. The middens and the beggars were cleared from the streets, a new unicorn was made for the mercat cross, and the magistrates kitted themselves out in new silk robes. Finally, the cleaners went through 'the haill palace' with 'ane puire manes heid [duster] for dichting doune the haill mouse webbis [cobwebs].'

In the end, Charles spent just one night at Linlithgow, on 1 July 1633. He was the last reigning sovereign to sleep in the palace.

Above: James VI in later life. After his succession to the English throne as James I, he visited Scotland only once, in 1617. At this time, he commissioned a new north range to replace the one that had collapsed.

Above: A decorative bronze hairpin found at Linlithgow Palace, dating from around 1630. It may have belonged to the hereditary keeper's wife, the countess of Linlithgow.

Top: The north range commissioned by James VI.

Opposite top: Cromwell at the Battle of Dunbar a few days before he occupied Linlithgow.

CROMWELL AND THE CIVIL WAR

A less welcome visitor to Linlithgow Palace was Oliver Cromwell in September 1650, shortly after his victory over the Scots at Dunbar.

During his Scottish campaign in the winter of 1650–1, Cromwell lodged in the palace. His 'roundheads' encamped on the peel, while his cavalry and their horses were accommodated in St Michael's Church. The troops set up artillery fortifications around the palace. In the process, they demolished the tolbooth, the mercat cross and the almshouse in the Kirkgate. This demolition was carried out mostly to secure supplies of stone, but also to give the gunners a clear field of fire.

Ten years later, Charles II was restored to the throne. The defences erected by Cromwell's forces were demolished and a new tolbooth built. Little was done to the palace, however. In 1668 it was described as formerly 'werie magnificent' but 'now for the most part ruinous'.

In 1678, the military draughtsman and antiquarian John Slezer drew the 'Prospect of Their Majesties' Palace of Linlithgow' (see page 37). His illustration depicts the palace still largely roofed. Just as well, for in the following year another royal visitor, James, Duke of Albany and York, stayed there while acting as commissioner to the Scottish Parliament on behalf of his elder brother, King Charles.

In 1685, the duke was crowned as King James VII and II, but he never returned to Scotland. When he fled into exile, the lights went out in the ancient palace of his Stewart ancestors at Linlithgow.

1633

CHARLES I
visits Linlithgow Palace during his only visit to Scotland.

1650–1

OLIVER CROMWELL
occupies Linlithgow, taking the palace as his own residence and erecting new artillery fortifications.

THE '45 AND THE FIRE OF '46

Above: A 19th-century engraving shows the destruction of Linlithgow Palace by fire in 1746.

Left: The memorial cairn at Culloden, where the Duke of Cumberland's forces eradicated the last hopes of the Jacobites, less than three months after the fire at Linlithgow Palace.

Linlithgow was to receive one final visit from a member of the royal Stewart dynasty. However, the triumphant arrival of 'Bonnie Prince Charlie' was a prelude to another devastating blaze.

The town of Linlithgow was thronged with people on Sunday 15 September 1745, eager to catch a glimpse of the handsome 25-year-old prince due to visit the palace that day. Prince Charles Edward Stuart, known as 'the Young Pretender', could not afford to linger, for he was making for Edinburgh, to reclaim Scotland's capital for the Stewart dynasty. Nevertheless, the palace fountain ran with red wine in the prince's honour.

By 1746, however, Prince Charles was heading for the Scottish Highlands once more, this time with a Hanoverian army hot on his heels. On 31 January, Charles' cousin, William, Duke of Cumberland, arrived at Linlithgow with over 10,000 government troops. Although most of the 'redcoats' encamped around the town, some bivouacked in the north range of the palace. As they marched out the following morning, a fire took hold in the north range. Molten lead dripping from the roof prevented the soldiers from extinguishing it. The palace was soon engulfed in flames once more. The fire may have been started deliberately by the departing troops. They may also have been responsible for some of the damage to the fountain and other masonry.

The Linlithgow magistrates did nothing to stop the blaze; they maintained they 'had no responsibility'. However, many of the townsfolk hurried to the scene and carried to safety what they could, much of it to their own homes! Despite the best efforts of the magistrates, not everything was returned.

Thus ended the glory of the royal palace of Linlithgow.

1745

PRINCE CHARLES EDWARD STUART
makes a fleeting visit to Linlithgow during his ill-fated campaign to restore the Stewart monarchy.

1746

WILLIAM, DUKE OF CUMBERLAND
occupies Linlithgow with a force of Hanoverian troops, on 31 January. The following morning, a fire engulfs the palace.

A PALACE FOR THE PEOPLE

The palace's long years as a magnificent royal residence had come to an end, but it remains an extraordinary and popular landmark and a focus for activity and discovery.

Since the fire of 1746, Linlithgow Place has remained uninhabited. Robert Burns, visiting in 1787, commented that it was 'a fine but melancholy ruin'. Although a variety of uses were suggested for the building – including as a prison of war for French soldiers during the Napoleonic Wars – it remained unused.

In 1853, the palace, peel and loch were entrusted into the keeping of Her Majesty's Commissioners for Woods and Forests, who transferred them to Her Majesty's Office of Works (now Historic Scotland) in 1874.

Today, the palace, peel and loch are alive once more, visited and enjoyed by townspeople and visitors, nature lovers, and a wide variety of local clubs and organisations. Historic Scotland has established a ranger service at Linlithgow to ensure that visitors to the peel have a safe and enjoyable visit.

The palace is a popular venue for weddings, and a variety of entertaining and educational events take place here. Costumed re-enactors including knights on horseback, poets, storytellers, musicians, dancers and falconers bring the palace and the royal park to life. In 2009, 120 costumed performers from all around Britain gathered at Linlithgow to re-create the atmosphere of the celebrations in 1503, when King James IV brought his new queen, Margaret Tudor, to the palace.

In their heyday, Linlithgow Palace and Peel were reserved for the enjoyment of a privileged few. Today, they can be enjoyed by everyone.

Bottom left: Costumed Junior Guides shelter from the rain between tours of the palace.

Bottom right: Kayaks and dinghies on the peel.

Above: Jousting on the peel – a spectacular revival of the sports enjoyed by the Stewart monarchs.

Above: Battle re-enactors revive old conflicts on the peel.

1787

ROBERT BURNS
visits Linlithgow Palace, which he describes as 'a fine but melancholy ruin'.

1853

LINLITHGOW PALACE
is placed in the keeping of HM Commissioners for Woods and Forests. It has remained in State care to the present day.

Linlithgow Palace is one of 26 Historic Scotland properties in the Lothians. A selection is shown below.

BLACKNESS CASTLE

Built in the 1440s and later repeatedly refortified, Blackness is a daunting and distinctive stronghold overlooking the Forth.

↗ 4 miles NE of Linlithgow

🕐 Open all year
Winter: closed Thu/Fri

📞 **01506 834807**

🚗 Approx. **4 miles** from Linlithgow Palace

CRAIGMILLAR CASTLE

Sited beyond Edinburgh's city walls, Craigmillar was a comfortable retreat for its noble owners and their royal guests.

↗ 2.5 miles SE of Edinburgh city centre

🕐 Open all year
Winter: closed Thu/Fri

📞 **0131 661 4445**

🚗 Approx. **20 miles** from Linlithgow Palace

CRICHTON CASTLE

Best known for its pyramid-pattern façade, unique to Scotland, this was the fashionable residence of the powerful Crichtons.

↗ 20 miles SE of Edinburgh City Centre off the A68

🕐 Open summer only

📞 **01875 320017**

🚗 Approx. **40 miles** from Linlithgow Palace

CAIRNPAPPLE HILL

Originally a henge monument, and later a burial site used over many centuries, Cairnpapple was a sacred place for some 5,000 years.

↗ 5 miles south of Linlithgow off the B592

🕐 Open summer only

📞 **01506 634622**

🚗 Approx. **5 miles** from Linlithgow Palace

For more information on all Historic Scotland sites, visit **www.historic-scotland.gov.uk**
To order tickets and a wide range of gifts, visit **www.historic-scotland.gov.uk/shop**

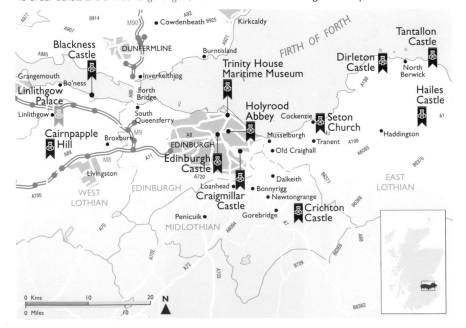

Key to facilities

Car parking	🅿
Bus/coach parking	🅿
Bicycle rack	🚲
Reasonable wheelchair access	♿
Toilets	🚻
Interpretive display	
Shop	🎁
Picnic area	
Self-serve tea and coffee	☕
Strong footware recommended	👢
Accessible by public transport	🚌